Fractions

1/4

1/2

BY SARA PISTOIA

Published by The Child's World®
1980 Lookout Drive • Mankato, MN 56003-1705
800-599-READ • www.childsworld.com

Acknowledgments
The Child's World®: Mary Berendes, Publishing Director
The Design Lab: Design
Editing: Jody Jensen Shaffer

Photographs ©: David M. Budd Photography

ISBN 9781623235291
LCCN 2013931430

Printed in the United States of America
Mankato, MN
July, 2013
PA02173

ABOUT THE AUTHOR

Sara Pistoia is a retired elementary teacher living in Southern California with her husband and a variety of pets. In authoring this series, she draws on the experience of many years of teaching first and second graders.

Fractions

People everywhere use **fractions**.
Fractions show how many **parts**
of something make up the **whole**.
Fractions can help us be fair
when we share.

The candy bar is a whole.

Let's cut it in two, right down the middle. Now there are two **equal** parts. Each part is a fraction called **one-half**.

one-half + one-half = one whole

5

Four friends have pie for dessert. How can they share it?

This way isn't very fair.

This way is better. Each friend gets **one-fourth** of the pie.

This pie is cut into fair shares. It has four equal parts, so everyone gets an equal piece.

Here are some other foods cut into parts.

This pizza is cut into three equal parts. Each part is **one-third**.

This apple is cut into two equal parts. Each part is one-half.

This pear is cut into two parts that are not equal. Neither part is one-half.

Is this sandwich cut into fractions?

Remember, a fraction must have equal parts. When you share, be fair! Use fractions.

Fractions can be equal parts of a group, too. You could share this group of six cookies with two friends. Don't forget yourself!

If you **divide** the cookies into three equal parts, each friend can have two cookies. Each person's share is one-third of the whole pile.

When bakers make cookies, they use fractions.

They use one whole egg.

They use one whole cup of flour.

But the rest of the ingredients are fractions:

one-half cup of sugar,

one-fourth cup of butter,

and one-half teaspoon of salt.

Here are some other fractions.

One-fourth of these flowers is pink.

What fraction of the flowers is yellow?

There are four flowers. Each flower equals one-fourth.

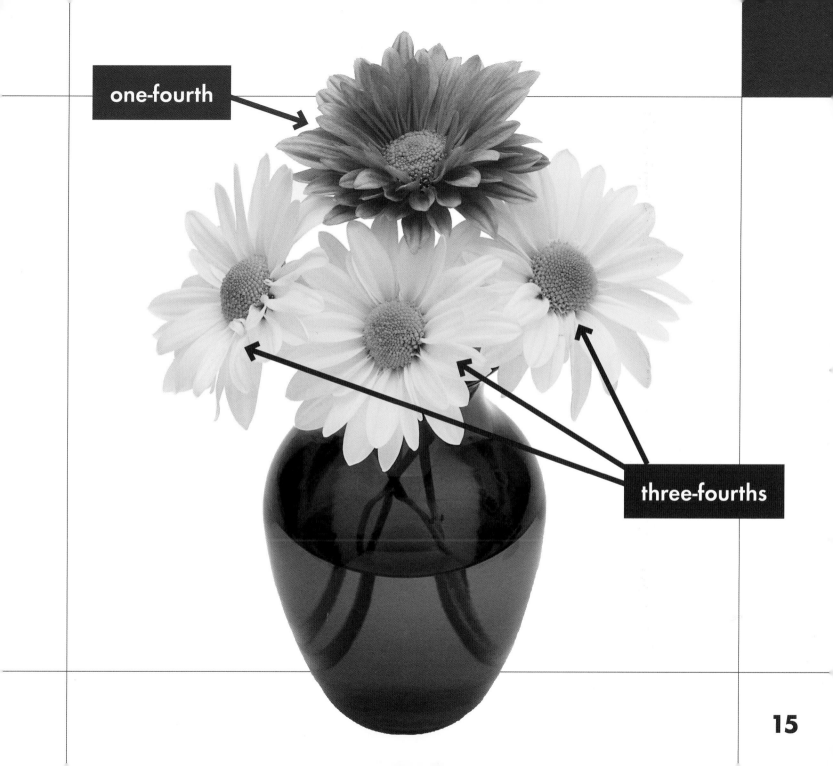

one-fourth

three-fourths

15

You can use words and pictures to talk about fractions. You can use **numerals**, too.

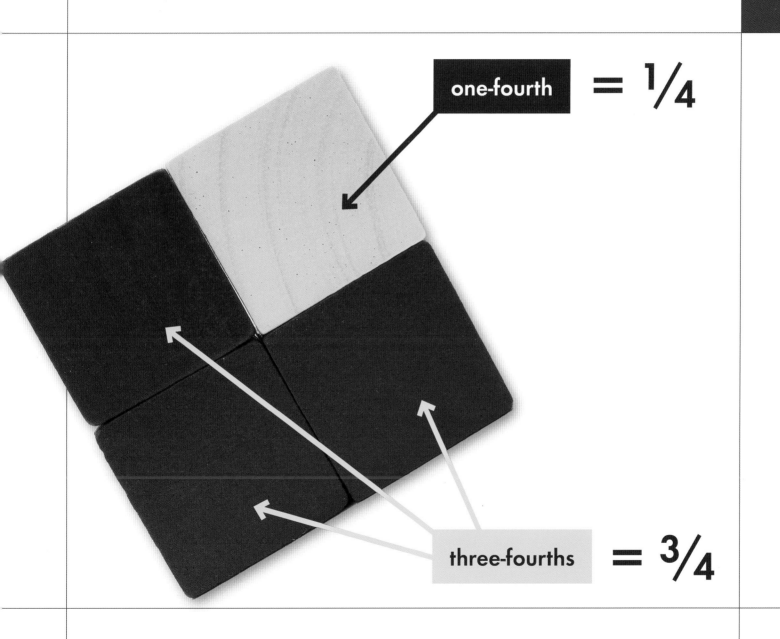

one-fourth $= \frac{1}{4}$

three-fourths $= \frac{3}{4}$

We often use numerals to show fractions.

The bottom numeral shows how many parts are in the whole thing. The top numeral shows how many parts we are talking about.

This stoplight has three parts. One light is on. The other two lights are off.

one-third $= \frac{1}{3}$

two-thirds $= \frac{2}{3}$

Here are ten bowling pins. A ball knocks down five pins. Five pins are still standing. What fraction of pins fell down?

There are two equal parts: five pins are standing and five pins have fallen. Each part is one-half of the whole.

So remember your fractions. Be fair when you share. Your friends will know just how much you care!

Key Words

divide
equal
fractions
numerals
one-fourth (¼)
one-half (½)
one-third (⅓)
parts
three-fourths (¾)
two-thirds (⅔)
whole

Index